Wayworn Wooden Floors

Wayworn Wooden Floors

Mark Lavorato

The Porcupine's Quill

Library and Archives Canada Cataloguing in Publication

Lavorato, Mark, 1975–
  Wayworn wooden floors / Mark Lavorato.

Poems.
ISBN 978-0-88984-351-6

  I. Title.

PS8623.A866W38 2012   C811'.6   C2012-901367-6

Readied for the press by Wayne Clifford.

Published by The Porcupine's Quill, 68 Main Street, PO Box 160,
Erin, Ontario NOB 1TO. http://porcupinesquill.ca

Represented in Canada by the Literary Press Group.
Trade orders are available from University of Toronto Press.

We acknowledge the support of the Ontario Arts Council and the
Canada Council for the Arts for our publishing program. The financial
support of the Government of Canada through the Canada Book Fund is
also gratefully acknowledged.

ONTARIO ARTS COUNCIL
CONSEIL DES ARTS DE L'ONTARIO

Canada Council   Conseil des Arts
for the Arts   du Canada

In Memory of Alden Nowlan

Table of Contents

This World

is the sprawling attic
of an abandoned building,
murmuring to its own musty heights.

Heirloom chests tucked into corners,
their tired lids clamping down
on maudlin keepsakes, worthy relics,
gradually dimming the meaning
of both.

Wayworn wooden floors lie
as if in wait for the dust to settle.
Sun melts through the windows
copper-plating the planks with tarnished
warmth. Shadows of leaves swim
over slats of maple, stretching
in spans of tongue-and-groove
that warp as slow as memory.
At night the moon heaves
pools of shadow around the room
like seas.

Dried wasps coil on the windowsills,
endowed, still, with a sting
for a tidying hand.

While the weighty ghosts that pass
over the ancient boards
trail a familiar sound, creak and bend
like some weathered song
we're sure we know
though can't quite remember
how it ends.

Woman Eating an Apple

Words for the lagging
November light of Sicily
always fail
but always try

It's a light that sketches
jagged lines along walls
that breathes shadow
into the blemishes
of plaster

It is a light that stretches
her lonely form across the floor
drawing her chair slanted, skeletal
mimicking her gestures
in blurry shapes
that bob between the cobblestones

It's a light that catches
the lime-green freckles
as she pares the apple
outlining the peels
like clumsy butterflies
which spill onto the plate
and dangle over its side
as if reaching out curious wings
towards the blue chequered cloth

A light that she holds her face up to
as if it were a wind
head leaning softly back
her shadow flailing out behind her
like a blowing shawl

That etches
the wrinkles of her hands
even deeper
that flashes the pink
of her open mouth
as she slips a grainy slice
between her lips

It is a light that lures her gaze
out into the middle distance as she chews
that abandons her to her thoughts
clouds over her expression
slows the movements of her jaw

It is a light that fails
to cast a glow
on the shadow of other days
but always tries

Sorry

Accidentally,
weed whacking in the garden this morning,
I decapitated one of your prize tulips.
Its petals a lovely arteriole-red,
veined in a cartilage-yellow.

The stem was severed neatly, cleanly; the head
lay serene in a basket
of grass clippings.

I carried it into your kitchen and left it there
floating in a bowl of water on the table
(a prominent corner of your kingdom)

just to make a point.

To You, Mrs. Woolf

You woke with a start, rising too quickly from a dream
that had you crawling backwards, away from something,
knees and palms pushing at the floor,
the ceiling pressing down until your head shoved through it
like a birth, strained and grimacing, arms unfolding into a light
you never asked to be washed in.

And in blinking the film of that dream away,
the receding haze held out an offering for focus,
not a room or table or familial washbasin,
but the tightening glimmer of an autumn forest.

The bedposts pinned down the flaking skin of tree roots;
the duvet's hem draping along a tapestry of pine needles.

Breath quickened, a shallow fluttering under the sheets,
which you clutched to your mouth in fists of wrinkled fabric;
allowing the flitting of your eyes to take in a world
that wasn't your own, and so, through the spectrum
of an untainted observation, became more your own
than its frenzied inhabitants, skittering along the branches,
filled with the vacancy of preparation,
the hint of snowflakes in their nostrils
so strong it emptied their eyes.

You held to a fragile calm long enough to watch
the delicate flames of a larch's fingers, still waxy with naissance
sprouting through knuckles withered tight
from a history that uncoiled into a measureless thread,
humming in the air.

Virginia, it was as natural
as every whirling process around you
that all you should want
was to go back
to sleep.

Happiness

A true story: Found a fox once
bright coil rusting in the spring grass

looked like it'd died in its sleep
its nose drowned in the fur of its tail

so I crouched down to touch
the still-glowing embers of its pelt

when, with a wild and frozen start, it woke up
I will never forget the electric green

of its eyes fixed to mine, and the
rushing sense that I was looking

into something I'd been scanning for
for miles or years or fathoms

and had found at precisely the moment
I wasn't prepared to, butterfly net in the closet

My need to swallow splintered the exchange
and with two bounds of flaming grace

it slipped through a slot in the long grass
the candle flame of its tail doused
into a thin wick of shadow

Must have stayed there an hour
wondering if he'd come back

A Handful of Seeds

My father teared at movies.
His hobby, though,
was taking life.

He told me once, excitedly,
convincing me to try it,
having gently pulled me into a corner
where no one could hear,
that it wasn't the hunt,
or the challenge, or the meat.
It was the killing.
To take a life from this world
just because you could.

He broke his leg one September,
so couldn't scour the hills
for savage creatures.
Instead, confounded,
he whittled a branch at
the edge of the forest,
his long cast pointing at the trees.

The autumn wind
fluttered through the clinging leaves
as they slowly
lost
grip.

And gradually, tenderly,
conversely,
he befriended the birds.

He sat for days
with a handful of seeds,
waiting.
And in time, though skittish with caution,
they came. First to the table beside him,
which was only a muffled drum roll away
from the safety of the branches,
and then, edging forward with tiny hops,
eyeing his cupped hand,
suddenly crouching, ready to fly
at the subtlest of movement.
Light feathered bodies
dainty with hollow bones,
hovering like spectators in a gallery,
wrists clasped behind backs,
scrutinizing this study of stillness,
of patience, of silence;
their shining black eyes
solemnly judging.

My father,
like the graveyard statue of a saint,
grinning at birds,
in sunlight as crisp as stone.

Later, his leg having healed,
he plucked his rifle from the corner again,
eager to tame the wild
that had come unleashed unto the world
in his absence.

Still, when I think of him,
it is this image that rises first.
A monument, honouring what he was,
but couldn't be.

Plea

I can't write today
the lids of my eyes pulling together
like lawn on either side of the sidewalk

Because of the neighbours living above
(not the old codger
but the couple with the sulky teenager
whose iPod is always seeping
from his ears with wires
an intravenous white)

It must have been his parents
pacing the hardwood floors
whittling away the soot-black
hours before dawn
back and forth
then in circles
endlessly treading

And the weathered joists
the corroded nails worming
out of the shrunken wood
had nothing better to do
than report the nuances
of their every
last
movement

Like the slowing of their steps
in front of the doorknob
Like their pleading with it
to turn

Three Colours

There are islands
on Superior's north shore
where wolves are forced to summer
marooned by the fracturing ice and
left to watch from the shores
as the shards recede and soften in the
water as black as pupils
Glacial-blue
irises

   blink

            The first is the caramel smear
            of cedar
            the bark peeling away
            from the pungent wood until
            the swirl of its grain
            blooms
            in the damp of drizzle

            The second is the colour of sunken granite
            with its embroidery of veins and fissures
            sloping beneath the inlet
            the surface glinting
            with the previous day's storm
            refracting an azure whose
            calm is tentative
            and bruised

The following morning
we understood why
seeing their tracks
padding along the beach
where we'd camped

The third is the dark
and chalky paste
on the roof of my mouth that night
suddenly awake
breath held
listening hungrily
to a silence that seemed
so palpably
to be listening back

Those
are the colours of your eyes
as you watch me now
and

blink

Oaxaca City

It rained music today
splashes tattering the street

I sought shelter under an archway
watching her wide four-year-old eyes
stare up through the shuffling of feet
moving in a dizzying array
of individual whims
in perfect unison

She was smiling
engrossed
long arms reaching down
swaying her from side to side
as if trying to stir
something innate
a pulse in her step that she has
and will remember
for the first time
one day

But for now, baffled
and spinning in laughter
she can do nothing
but shield her head
with ecstatic hands
from the downpour

Postcards

stamp the fridge shamelessly
with colours brash enough to appease
the imagination
and boards of tourism

Having a
Here
Wish you were
Weather
Thinking of
Great time

The pen clicks shut
gritty with sand
cocktail umbrellas swabbing
maraschino dye
like a stab wound
'Please
can we just …'
A palm flashed like a badge
holiday police
detaining old arguments
into the corners
of new suitcases

But how they dangle now
against the white lacquer
magnet pinned
something to push our faces against
in ungainly silences
Golf-greened ruins
Aborigines sat in studios
Landmarks you could
shake a snowstorm in

And they stare back at us
accusingly
orthogonal eyes beaming
clumped in clusters
of either too few
or too many

Conflict Resolution

Worked in a ski chalet one winter, penniless
but tucked into my cramped bedspace by snowdrifts.
As luck would have it, around the table one night
I got to talking to a professional conflict resolutionist.
I asked him the obvious question, about Israel and Palestine.
How would you resolve that, professionally?

Easily, he replied. We all want the same thing.
This, he had said, was the most important aspect
of conflict resolution: To understand that we always,
all of us, want the same thing. To be safe. Children.
Food. Warmth. Shelter. A vote. Education. Free speech.
Empathy, he held, was nothing but a simple and short walk away.
If he could have all of Israel and Palestine around a single table,
the two nations lining a giant Formica surface,
he could fix the whole mess in an hour. Maybe less.

He was clearly a professional.

I liked the man. So it's a pity I didn't know
it was his daughter I was buying drinks for,
later on in the pub, while penniless.

The next morning, realizing the gaucheness of my error,
I tried to talk to him about the weather, with little success,
citing the impeccable forecast, listing off the
centimetres expected, temperatures at different elevations,
wind direction, cloud types, probably
trailing off with the dew point.

In the nostril-breathing quiet that ensued
we both looked out the window for snowflakes. Both of us
wanting the same thing.

The Morning after the Canadiens Lost

It was raining in Montreal, off and on, trailing
cloudlets hanging low, dragging their heels.

Out of coffee, I made my way through sober streets
where car horns were tight-lipped and banners had

suddenly vanished into hockey-closet air, when
I saw a man on des Érables getting into his car,

contemplating the removal of the Habs flags from
his rooftop; spires draping now, outlandish and sodden.

Most of the time, most of us are guilty of being
fair-weather fans, friends, cousins, sons. But not

on this street, not today. With a nod of conviction,
he gently shuts his door and pulls away, the polyester

flapping limp and heavy, pointing backwards, singing
the quiet song of our defeat, a one-float parade, streamers

clapping clumsy for our failure. An anthem held up
less high, less brazen. Fallible, fallen, and beautiful.

Vézère

We were crammed in like organ pipes
eyes to the ceiling, mouths open
paying no attention to the guide shuffling by
or to his hand
reaching behind a shadowed rock
to switch off the lights

There was a stiff
motionless
silence

Then the sudden flick of a lighter
which brought the cave walls
trembling to life

Charcoal outlines rearing with liquid muscle
Ochre eyes still white with fear

Yet what I felt
(a cold finger dragging across the nubs of my spine)
wasn't something ancient and familiar
wasn't a thread-thin legacy
tracing its way back
through air, sediment
through blood

but rather a deficiency
an overwhelming absence
Not, I think, of ceremony
or tradition
or even of faith
But of sacredness

Five Perspectives of a Church

Bell

Its chime weakening as it spreads
like ripples in a wide pond
with islands of yellow water lilies
villages blooming in the night
It gives a slow and heavy nod
to the people in the distance
listening, counting the hours
of their sleeplessness
It is a nod that is at once
courteous, noble, knowing
One to the woman standing
in her kitchen with the lights off
to her pills and her glass of water
One to the teen at her lamp reading
into the romances she's sure to have
to the paragon couple on the cover
And one to the man watching his ceiling
wondering, again tonight, if this
is the way that prayers
are answered

Mouse

With her second litter of the year nursing
             it was the teeming hunger that led her
too far astray from her usual rounds
             Which is where she found it
block of endlessly delicious poison
             filling her cheeks to a stretch
She didn't realize the mistake as much
             as she did the drunkenness, the
wobbling nave she found herself under
             for the very first time, usually
keeping to the dowdy edges of lint balls
             and dust, skirting the hardwood trim
in only the deepest candle flicker of night
             But now there seemed to be stained-glass
light everywhere above, a scraggly hunch of fur
             breathing faster than a panicked pulse
swimmingly lost in the holy wooden open
             Her burgundy blood thinning to water
she feels herself spreading, blurring, dividing, as if
             beside herself, there were another, equal
presence there, easing her gently to her side

Cornerstone

Its composition the remnants
of a seabed burial, of brine-
silt snowflakes blanketing the dark
Bulbs of algae falling
as slow as angels
trumpeting shells
of molluscs that shatter from the
gargantuan weight at leaden depths
Embalming the dead in calcium,
mummifying slender skulls, teeth, joints
into a cement of ocean creatures that
will in time be deemed sacrosanct
enough to quarry, cleave, hew

All things, when pressed tightly enough
make a sound; this one
a dense murmur
subsonic hymn of stillness
Clamped at the edge of the high tower
it has deliberated its shape for centuries
And the ghosts of innumerable
instincts have come to disagree
tending towards something less
quadratic, less human, contrived
Collectively, and drawing from the
ashen nucleus of patience at each of
their centres, they begin to will the angles
away, flexing their crumbling muscle

Janitor

it's not a great job he knows what with
the meagre pay and surface area
of a gymnasium having to wax the
floors run a dusting rag over and
under the book boxes on the pews not
to mention all the kitsch statues with acrylic
blood oozing from their ribcages and
foreheads sometimes the sweeping
alone takes hours his arms swinging
tired a quick-draw bottle of windex dangling
from his belt by the trigger and then
there's the times he eyes the old women
whispering into their thumbs and it strikes
him as depressing that so much in this
cold and airy dim is said with no
one listening on the other end and that
gets him thinking about the echoes in the
high arches when he drops his mop the way
the sound curves around forever like light in
space and what if that was what happened to
all the wishes the focus the will of those words
not quite spoken in this place and then he has to
slouch on a pew windex on the wood beside him
and look up into that murky quiet that everyone who
enters strains to assert but which like a cupped ear
can never have you noticed ever quite hold
its own silence

Swallow

A winter of dryness
                desert of saturate light
Fists of scrub shaking at the sand
    of a waterless beach
            wide as an ocean
                    buckling its grainy folds
                    into silken shadows
            It's only the odd insect rustling
                the air that she lives on
dreaming in shivering time-lapse
            of her nesting place
                    a moon's flight to the north
        Where lichen scorches the stone
            of the belfries and every evening
    the leafy horizon drains the sun of its rust
In the sleep of her hollow bones she remembers
            generations of sweeping turns
                    through the gusts that eddy the steeple
            landing on the mud lip of a future nest
        that she can somehow already feel
        knows the invisible weight of
    Like the pull of the compass in her skull
Like belief

To Mrs. Koran

You had a shelf near your desk crammed with
poetry anthologies, only one with enough prints
to be handed out, twice during the week-long unit
that made eyes roll and bodies slump
sneakered legs sprawling beneath desks
in protest

The rest were single copies you collected over the years
some with your name scribbled into the cover
bought out of your own pocket
sifting through reduction bins and
flea market tables

I'm here to tell you that it was me
I stole them, one of each

and read them covetously before bed
my mother asking from the other side of the door
what I was doing
when I would straighten up, shutting the book
and lie

There were some I didn't understand, but tried
straining my eyes as if with a
flashlight under the covers
bent on the code and its method
amateur cryptography that
floated words across the blackboard
of my sleep

Mrs. Koran, I'd like to apologize for robbing
your future students of these poems
(themselves stolen words
pilfered from the lives
that drift along our plundered soil)
Yes, I'd really like to say that I'm sorry
But I'm not

Google Earth

They've come up with something you'd love,
Heinz, a 3-D interactive map of the world, with
real-time weather no less. You can pan through
at any latitude, any angle, gliding along possible
routes and ridges in a way that used to be
confined strictly to the imagination. So you
know, I zoomed in on the summit you fell from,
saw how steep the slope was, how rough the
terrain where you landed. And after that, I typed
in my own address, watching the land fall away,
lifting like a javelin breath of helium, the globe
smoothly spinning, slipping daylight hours off
into the endless dark, and sinking earthward
again, wedging through the provinces, through
my city's streets, right into my backyard, where
it slowed to a hovering halt, just above my roof,
as if with a long and wary step, you could set
foot onto the shingles there, laughing your
greetings as you hopped down onto my fence.
And let it be known that if you ever did, my
friend, I wouldn't waste a second; that I'd grab
us both a beer, sit down on the grass, and fill you
in on some of the things they've come up with
since you've been gone. Though I imagine we'd
soon revert to what we'd always done when
catching up, and I'd ask you to tell me all about
your last journey.

Dawn

I imagine the soul
if there is such a thing
as a dawn

As a slow seed of grey
sketching the horizon
swirling the clouds

The bristle of leaves
feathers unfurling
the rustle of colourless life
as it stirs
flutters, calls out

And this sound and movement culminate
building, swelling with light
until the sun, at last
its edges abrupt and wavering
breaches the skyline
with a perfect
and absolute
silence

Sundays

This morning I want to raise my cup
watch the steam curl in the sun
that melts through the glass
cutting hazy shapes on my floor
And I want to whisper:
To Sundays

To the days when we find ourselves
sitting at windows like dogs
chins on the sills, watching
waking to a world whose eyes are half open

When the hours shuffle past unclocked
the hiss and hum of cars ebbing, a tide gone out
people walking at its edge in languid steps
either in pairs or alone

Birds fall from branches
fluttering to the ground like leaves
And the trees seem to stop and hang in the air
as if they're waiting for something
something we can't even guess at
and don't

We notice the clouds for the first time in weeks
tugging across the sky
craning their necks to look down
or up, in some direction
where we have no weight

Which has me lifting this glazed cup
that dangles at the end of my arm
Here's to the sounds of feeling blessed
to the slow, muffled quiet

D

I am stuck to you
like the stamp on an envelope
of one of those letters we write and never send
licked with a teary tongue
and slapped onto the corner with reckless abandon
that decayed as fast as courage

One of those letters written in frantic sentences
words trying desperately to convey things that were never said
but should have been
The type of letter that sits in a drawer until it's forgotten
which is never
and that ends with:

Come home.
Even if I don't know where that is.
I've seen it.
I have seen it.
It's the place where the sun drags slow across the floor
like it's sneaking up on us;
skulking over the wood while you read on your stomach,
crawling with hunted silence
towards your bare feet.

Please.
Meet me there.

Please.

Maps of Antiquity

Back when the world had edges
and was fringed with tentative shores,
rivers squiggling inland where the ink ran
dry for want of their sources, there were people –
and always for the most illogical reasons –
who set out into that landscape of whiteboard
uncertainty, where every rise or crest ahead
concealed unimagined pitfalls, or some epic
creature of myth; their steps having to tread
the absurd line between petrified and bold.
That is where I feel I am walking
with you.

Rose

was a black Labrador retriever named
after the town in Alberta where she was born,
Rosemary, which had a main street of gravel.

Her intelligence was prodigious,
made Lassie look as dumb as a stick.
She could understand whole sentences
of instructions, and hunted with an intuition
that was, by all accounts, uncanny.

I used to torture her by telling her
to sit, stay, then throw a ball
into a corner of the yard, get down
on all fours, and whisper into her ear,
fffffetid. A twitch. Every fragment
of her focus on the ball as taut
and trembling as her body, bent
on the command to trigger
into a sprinting blur of black
as if projected through the lagging
smoke of gunpowder. She waited, strung,
cocked, loaded, my friends elbowing each other
with suppressed laughter.
Ffffennigan.

One night, in one of my favourite places
in this world, she asked to be let out
and found a spot in the grass
to lie down and put her bones
to rest. Years later I had a vivid
black and white dream of her there,
a chinook blowing the meadow
into wild swirls, clouds roiling dark.

She woke up and came to me, her eyes
all wood-grain sympathy, and spoke
in a kind of voice that sang silent
in my head, and she said that everything,
everything was *all* right. Then
she returned to her chosen spot
in the field, and the dry grass
closed in around her, whirling
to perfectly consume her again.

I have wondered about the message.
Which sounds much like the lie
we use to assuage others
not quite as clever
as we are.

True Patriot Love

Rain falls in steel streamers
soaking the flag
with its serrated leaf
blushing in the glow
of stadium lights

While below
parking-lot lines
slope to a centre
and droop with the
tarmac weight of histories
we've turned away from
Yellow paint
glimmering with water
that sloughs away
like a tired skin

And something
at the end of its tether
is tinging at the flagpole
like it doesn't know
there's no one listening
a rhythm that is crude and earnest
and sinking down
into the dotted puddles
A chiming that tells
of laced blankets
and interment letters
of sunken pendants
and chords from
the old country

that were lost
under our gravestones
which ease against the dirt
as if they were
the tightening baffles
of an accordion

And it is this song
this song
that is infinitely
more
beautiful
than the one we know

Vertigine

In memory of Alfonso Lavorato

Whenever they move him
he screams
body tensed
fingertips groping frantically
for an edge
he never manages to catch

> The nurses lift on three.
> One. A traded glance, hands twisting into cloth.
> Two. The blanket suddenly taut, his eyes begin searching
> wildly between the fuzz of lights
> for the onslaught
> of panic.

Three.

His shouts are those of a child lost
into tumbling air
an exponential wind
streaming up from the ground
as the details of the terrain sharpen
with each
passing
second

Sometimes
he hollers the names of his brothers
all dead and inhumed
as if imploring them to open their graves
pillow his impact with
a crater of ashes

An efficient whirl of hands replaces diapers, new sheets,
pull, tuck, continence pad, catheter insertion,
swap glistening yellow bag for empty one, check watch,
timed interval for turning patient over, prevent excessive reddening
of underside with the same commonsensicality one would apply
to meat on a rotisserie.

1955 left
his wife and two children alone in Calabria
landlubber vomiting across the Atlantic
the only fresh air on deck
spitting drops into his face
saltier than tears
While the hiss and flutter of the hull blade
sliced a string of foam through
an endless landscape of
blue-black hills

In a silence only brothers know
they travelled west for a week
by train, jobless
the clunk-cla-clunk hypnotism
of lake-sheen and blurry trees
streaking the windows

He lived in a boxcar for two years
counting pennies
at the end of the prairie
where the bottom-jaw teeth of the mountains
sever its grainy tongue
The wind a thistle sandblast
shuddering the rusted leaf springs
Sleep thin and fidgety
curling against the
steel-drum
echoes

Ward calm again, patient pushing pedals
of wheelchair like he's in a vehicle and gliding
through a black-ice curve on a canyon road,
both feet locking up the brakes.

When he'd saved enough money
he wired his family three
tickets on a cargo ship
and began
his slow
climb
up

Listening to the rail workers'
private inventories of
how many bodies had
cartwheeled through the air
from the local high-level bridge
incited by the sluggish
approaching trains
An accidental slip
a listless roll over the side
a dive of unfaltering conviction
the distant earth welcomed them all

    Patient has wormed down chair, feet having
    slipped off, neck crooked and atrophied.
    Nurses circle, organize, nod, while
    my father crouches to explain in dialect
    concept of lifting only few inches,
    just until sitting straight again.
    Okay, Papá?
    No answer.

On three.

And we
strangers to him now
grandson, nephew, daughter
watch like second-class passengers
from the observation car
as he drops away
again
tracing his long path to the ground
with a shriek that
claws at the wind

Falling
in the only way one can
inconsolably
alone

Recordar

is the verb *to remember* in Spanish

With little mutation from its Latin origin, it means, literally:

    to pass, again, through the heart

If there is a truth, it lies

in our constant reinvention of it

Every word ever written

is fiction

Necessary, pulsating, wondrous

                            fiction

There is a bench

in front of a lake I know, at just the spot
a bench should be. The view from it is one
of my renditions of perfect; while the bench
is not. The planks are weathered and grey, given
to stinging fingers with a sliver when dragging
over the wood to brush away fallen leaves or pips.
One of the sides has succumbed to frost heave,
and over long periods of time, one can notice
the slow pull of one's body down the skew.
This shoddy foundation once got me thinking
about the municipal workers who installed it,
digging and cement mixing, shovels expertly
funnelling the mix of gravel and sand into the hole
which someone hadn't dug quite deep enough.
When they returned to bolt the planks into place
I can easily imagine one of them, not saying it but
noting in his mind, how this bench was situated
at just the spot a bench should be; maybe
even imagining that he'd come back sometime
for one of those picnics he was always promising.
Of course, I don't know if he ever did. What I
do know is that tonight the snow is falling heavily
outside, crystalline parachutes settling gently onto
everything under the churning clouds. The storm
is silent, patiently accumulating, mushrooming surfaces,
cloaking the definition of objects. Like the bench I know,
looking out onto a lake, abandoned and in the dark
for now, as another layer, and another, is softly added
onto one of my renditions of perfect.

Fingerpaintings

I

Wearing an old university sweater he found
in a box under the stairs, he spoons Tupperware
leftovers between his teeth, staring ahead while
beads of dark slide down the window to his right,
indicating, it would seem, that
                    It's raining
                            outside,
the wet roads doubling every brake light that slows
in the traffic, where, he calculates, his soon-to-be ex
is almost certainly stuck and waiting, tapping
the steering wheel to the radio, off-time, in that way
she does. He's only here till he finds a place,
until then it seems
                    It's pouring
                            over childhood
memorabilia and yearbook regrets, the glow-in-the-
dark stars he stuck to his ceiling two decades ago
still above but now only giving off a paltry glimmer,
the bowman of his favourite constellation having
withered into the last two holes of its belt. He
imagines that his mother's in her bed reading
while
        The old man
                    is watching television
in a volume that rattles the cabinets, the screen burning
at the blue of its wick. While the cataract dog that used to
bound alongside him on his jogs in high school kicks
in her basket, ecstatically unaware of every hardship that exists
in married life; as well, it would seem, as the fact that she

is snoring

II

And to think how convinced that pudgy landscaper was –
with his dented truck and idiot son – that these stones
would best be set in an oval. Lucky for her she was
adamant; the way she is when she knows she's right.
Because now, her special-ordered riverbed granite,
fist-sized and hand-selected for the optimum ratio
of feldspar and quartz, circuits the hedge in
an absolutely perfect
                    Ring around the roses

Which is, of course, the shape that most cleanly
complements the tight angles she keeps so fastidiously
pruned, strolling through her yard with a pair of clippers.
Like this evening, snipping a rogue leaf from one
of the shrub's flushest lines before stepping back
to admire the rest of the garden, dragging her eyes,
slowly, from one earthenware pot of flowers to the next,
pausing to relish each colourful cluster individually, even
imagining what some of them resemble. Like this one,
with its likeness to a champagne glass after the first pour,
a foam of chrysanthemums chasing the liquid up the flute.
Or that one, as if from the brimming pouch
of a flower thief, a
                    Pocket full of posies

She understands how important this is, the conscious
appreciation of her property. It isn't so much the owning
of decadence as it is the understanding of what it's worth;

the recognition that you've been working hard at something,
while others haven't. She slips off her shoes and opens
the veranda door, clicking her tongue at the film of dust
on the frame, as grey and powdery as the
                                    Ashes, ashes

of her father in a tight-lidded urn, perched in an alcove
upstairs across from a painting he once rolled his eyes at.
In the same way she had done an hour ago, sighing
at the clock and pouring another wee drop of single malt
to nurse in silence. Which isn't as much silence as it is
grandfather-clock-ticking, which becomes more insistent,
tallying the minutes she's waiting up again,
alone with the imaginings of the flawless though ditsy
body he's likely running his hands over. And with
the sensation that the hardwood floors are beginning
to sway, she returns with the bottle this time, clopping her
tumbler onto the glorious relic of her end table, sinking
her sea legs into the cushions, assuring herself that
nights like these happen to everyone. Even Cynthia
across the street, waving her daughter off to the bus stop
with her practised head tilt and milky nail polish
(the pompous bitch). Yes. Even her.
Every now and then
                    We all fall down

III

It was Einstein said we'd fight
the Fourth World War with
                    Sticks and stones
Clearly in the know,
having worked on that mushrooming
knowledge of perfect decimation that's since
become a science unto itself; a progress,
development, advancement, words
it's true, I don't
tend to think
            Will break my bones but
                        let's
not kid ourselves here, somewhere along
the way we've swapped mongering propaganda
for PR firms and doctors of spin, with
letterings so surgical they're almost poetic –
Fat Man, Patriot, Smart, Little Boy – every one
of them contentedly chipping away at my suspicion
that it's only their
            Names will never hurt me

IV

The guards assigned a misfit
to give the tour, antsy woman
all fingers, doling out new words
for everyday things, the semantics
of cleaving the outside world from the in –
Bone Yard, Chain, Sallyport, Pruno –
the few she caught she didn't need

Here's the laundry, cleanest place
in the Industry Area, and

Here's the church

fluorescent-bulbed for multi-
denominational reflection
painted with a dull quiet
that peels from the walls
Out into the Yard with its
faraway sky, framed in brick

And here's the steeple

of sorts, watchtower spiring
with bug eyes of tinted glass
Handed off to a guard to return
to her cell, they got stuck in a block
for unsettling minutes
buzzing for someone to

Open the doors

When her bars finally rang shut
she lay on her cot, blinking at the paint
that peeled from her roof like quiet
finding it was as if she'd stared too long
at the sun, the night that landed her there
branded to her retina, the way everyone
was striding so sovereign along the street
before it happened, their naive
silhouettes still smouldering
She wonders if it'll be like this for years
to come, that she'll just close her eyes

And see all the people

V

Hate can twist its way into everything,
wringing my stomach tight
with even the thought of you
whose head I once balanced
in the crook of my arm, whose back
I have dragged my mouth across
The mouth that never quite thickened
with the courage enough
to call you out as the

Liar, liar
            that you are
with your palm-leaf eyes
and their shivering way of saying
everything you don't
I have sometimes shocked myself
with the want of watching you suffer
Of standing by, out of reach and pitiless
while you, with an oasis in sight
though a touch too far off,
kerosene doused, with
your shirt and

Pants on fire
            flailing towards the shore
without a matchstick's hope
in hell

A daydream
conjured to comfort
until the moment I see you
with a bag of groceries on the street
and it all unravels, fraying in the way
that singed eyelashes might, being replaced
with the vision of you following me
home, unwinding our scarves to

Hang them up
             over our coats like we used to
But all you offer is to meet for lunch next week
saying that you'll call and winking a smile
that has me gliding dangerously over the
sidewalk home, puttering on the fuel
of forgiveness, which will very likely
snuff out as the days pass, eyeing
the receiver, again dangling
all my stupid hope

On a telephone wire

Arriving First

He raises a lantern,
squints into the night.
How, it seems,
the grass slithers;
while the dark,
pressing its wide face
against the lamp glass,
opens its mouth
and breathes
the lightest
measured
breath.

He steps back, shakes his head,
remembering the blur of Johannes'
hands sweeping above the beer steins,
his urgency magnetic,
drawing the chairs in ever closer,
until the table hovered with heads,
whispering, nodding.
Because what he'd said was true,
mostly. Mostly.

The flicker of flame
approaches from behind,
a swath of men
shoulder to shoulder.

He watches his long bobbing shadow
shrink,
then swallows,
barbs scratching along the length
of his throat.

They move forward together,
toward the sleeping house,
the grass at their feet
slithering.

Geese

There are things that are pure, that nothing can spoil;
bloody, sure, but not mar, not blemish. Like the hunters
I overheard talking about their blinds and decoys,
shotgun barrels dark as cattails, rising from tufts
of clipped reeds and bulrushes.
                                When life-pairs
of geese glide low over the fields to spend the night
in the marshes, you can down just one of them,
with a wing shot perhaps, a slow spiral out of the dusk
while she or he gawps around, trying to work out
the tragic riddle. The mate, it's said, will circle,
distraught and unhinged, and eventually

return into the ambush, flashes of lead pellets
and pinprick thunder, jeers of success.

Or like the news tonight, when another gunman
went pacing through another restaurant,
and the daughter of a retired couple
slipped through a broken window, quietly
gesturing for her mother to follow. And how

that woman stood in those glimpses of fresh air,
with her husband beyond any means of help
on the floor behind her, but turned
just the same to walk back
and meet him there.

Aerial Calculations

for Imad Buali

He's decided to move back to Saudi for good.
Tired, he says, of the typecasts in the news, film,
of being seen as the Evil Arab, watching,
distrustful, edgy, as the world gathers and stares
as if wanting to stare through
bulletproof glass.

He pauses the DVD of his latest trip home
to explain the seagull standing in his parents' garden,
found one morning by the groundskeeper, its wing
broken from an aerial miscalculation. It didn't cower
when a merciful hoe was raised above its head,
just blinked.

But the gardener couldn't bring himself to do it,
and so returned with some bread, as he would every day
for years to come. The gull's wingtip dragging over
the paving stones, pinions frayed and stringy with dirt;
the enclave's sandy corners stamped with webbed tracks
and the trailing squiggles of its endless
calligraphy.

Pressing play again: the bird, unsure of this documentarist,
circles with smooth steps, orbiting the camera, watching
distrustful, edging closer to the walls, ever further,
as if riding the seaside thermals of its earlier days,
when an invisible buoyancy had lifted it with a lightness
greater, even, than the way we imagine freedom
to feel.

Flight Path

There's always at least one in the sky here,
streamlined metal gleaming out of the blue
the way a surface-skimming fish might, seen
from the eyes of a bottom-feeder.

Planes gliding ahead of the invisible rumble,
towing their singed blurs along, vapour
stretching so thin it disappears behind
the sailing glints of spider thread.

While inside the passengers shift and slouch
armrested and reclining in the stratosphere.
Headphones competing with the burr of the turbines;
conversations stubbed out, gazes rise to the no-smoking light.

Carry-on baggage in the overhead compartments clinking
with duty-free forties and twice-X-rayed rolls of dental floss.
Inflight magazines worth three haphazard flips, tucked back into
the seat-pocket, behind vomit bags that stiffen with a queasy pale.

Where, for the paranoid and first-timers, white knuckling
their gripping novels, every crying baby is a potential oracle;
leaning into their portholes to eye the rivets outside,
streaks of grease dragging over the wings

by an inconceivable wind, which shudders the fuselage well
into the night, nuggets of sleep clotting corners of eyes,
waking too long in recirculated air, glimpsing down
as the islands of streetlights float past, unnameable.

Which is where I'm harboured, sipping my wine
in the summer dark, watching the red and green lights
blink out on the horizon, the jet-grumble fading into
rusty-hinged cricket song, until the next slow

billowing thunder rises from the opposite skyline,
paving another dusty road through the constellations,
prying the meridian open with its beam,
somehow shooting sure of where we're going to, and shy

of where we've been.

Present

We both know I've left you before,
and without a thought really, for another
place with longer shadows I'd visited, or
some mountain range I've always wanted to;
running my hands over orchid-smooth skin.
While you stayed right here, continuing on
without judgement or bitterness, without
anything but yourself, which of course changes
every time I go away; though always, somehow,
for the better; and often even having placed, in your
haphazard way, somewhere in my periphery,
and sometimes right beneath my nose,
a gift.

Harbour Seal

I was sitting at a point where the two channels sway
into every lunar flux, sluggish waters flailing
branches of seaweed in their black wind

when its head breached the surface with a rippleless rise
whiskered curiosity seeming to listen more with
the flaring of its nostrils than the pinpricks of its ears

Resurfacing in wary intervals, sewing a perimeter
it drank me in with the wet of its inky eyes
a wordless interview that I was sure to fail

and did, finding myself suddenly alone and leaning out
over the edge where the clamped mouths of barnacles
breathe silver bubbles and sink away into the dusty dark

past bulbs of yawning tentacles and sea snails tracing
their gradual increments, while I thought about
the exchange, this glimpse, for both of us, into a phantom

world we'll never understand, and yet is close enough
that we can dip a part of ourselves into, as if with
the feeble and sinking effort of trying to reach across

The Old Woman Living Opposite

Sometimes in the shed, aspen shoots
tendril through the floorboards,
suckered from rhizomes and stretching
their spines up to the cool glass.

Behind them spiders gather the corners
holding grease-still air
that only stirs when someone slips
inside for a garden tool, or once a year
for the tangled barbed wire of Christmas lights,
the closing door rifting waves
through the dusted fabric of cobwebs.

Teetering stem with a single leaf
towering pale over grey joints
wrinkled as sagging knees,
having reared its head in what it senses
is the wrong place, yet the only place
it knows.

Where the sole thing left to do is
perch the point of its chin on the sill
and draw what it can from the day;
even snatching the paltry sustenance
from every glint that shifts
in the night.

Uschi

Remember how, that September, we walked every evening
from the cabin at the edge of the mountains, and how
that one night we happened on all those buffalo
just before dark, corralled by a sturdy electric fence,
huddling in the ravine furthest from us? And
the discussion we had when we saw the culvert
passing under the barrier's clicks of alternating current,
weighing out the pros and cons of using it as a crawlspace
until we were inching through to the other side
over the dried mud and twigs, hands running along the
dark corrugations of metal? And how we stole through
the pasture, heads low, sure that, with nowhere to run,
they'd trample us if they spooked, finally slinking on our
bellies to peek over a rise, only to find them so close
we could smell their woolly curls, enormous humps of
live weight compacting the clay, dusty nostrils sighing?
Do you remember how everything at that moment,
how every being framed inside the enclosure
slowed into a careful stillness; how every eye paused
to ruminate on the falling dusk and its shadowless forms,
the grass holding the damp of its breath, while the sky
lifted evenly, growing thinner, dissolving into the first stars?
And how the air all around us, in every direction,
was humming? Do you remember, Uschi, wondering
if it was the electric fence we were hearing, or something
else, something that was pulsing its way through everything,
everything that is wild and raw and true?
Do you, Uschi? Do you?

Sierra de Chuacús

'For thirty-five years
none of this was safe.'
His hand sweeping along the skyline
then sinking
moon-slow
into the tiny plaza

I listened, nodding
like I understood the meaning
of regime thugs and rebels corrupted
of mines peppering orchard lanes
and the olive skin of children
wilting from sleeves and ankle hems
new grass swirling their clothes
into its tangled embroidery

When it ended
these villages were voiceless, still
doors open to empty kitchens

Which the government filled
with the jobless from the city
plates still in cupboards
drawers pulled clanking

'That's why they seem so content.
Because they should be.'

And when the two boys sprang
from behind the fountain
one of them running
the other kneeling
to line up the sights
of his fingers and arm
we both looked away
before the staccato
Bam

Where He Put Them

Isn't it strange how light collects,
gathers in the quietest puddles,
inside the shoes of someone
who is gone?

Novembrance Day

I

The cenotaph that begged to differ
when I stepped off the path
I trod every evening
outside a village in Austria
The shrine was flower-wreathed and cast
with names, dates, places; the font rubbed green
from the dragging thumbs of rain

Standing on knots of ivy
the silence lent itself to imaginings
of rifle reports and command lines
where soldiers slipped from their lives
as easily as lead from the steel of casings
Sniper fire popping out of flashes in the dark
bursts of soil crowning the meadows
bare hands clamped down over armoured helmets
too scared to remember
to pray

The commemoration was a common one
the standard plaque and obelisk
until I realized the iron crosses
Axis stigmas stamping the stone
their emblems pointing out
that these were the soldiers
who'd been picked off
by the ones I'd been taught
to mourn

II

'These seeds had evidently lain in the old chest since about the year
1195.... Some of them were planted in a hothouse and carefully watched.
They sprouted and bloomed and proved to be poppies.'

The New York Times
December 8, 1901

I've lived where they spring from ditches
building sites, demolition mounds,
weed-bulbs floating crimson above
lumps of disturbed earth
and the driest of loam.

Their stems wizened fingers
pointing at the ground
in an unsteady sway,
the weight of a bee enough
to camber a swoon.

The truth about their seeds lying
dormant for epochs adds a twist
to their exploited symbolism,
when the moment they held their breath
began long before the age of gasmasks.

Waking from another time
shaking the scarlet fists of a different battle
a different peace, and dropping clusters
of germ to be overturned in another
distant future.

Where they will blossom once more
into perfect memories
with a colour that hurts,
in a precision that we
will never be able
to echo.

Abandoned Farm

The sound of the wind is defined
only by what it blows through:

Wheatgrass, timothy, foxtail, sweeping
the slopes and undulating
like a horizontal flag
at half mast;

through the loops of barbed wire
that spring from the grass to dive in again,
suturing the wound
of a fallen fence;

or the grey splinters of window frames,
and the glossy fingernails of glass
hollowing them out;

the burr oak that so stubbornly
wouldn't take in the shelter belt
now covering one of the children's rooms,
the trunk at the foot
of where the bed
once was;

and the caragana
brought over from the old country
(which is flourishing, yellow flowers
shivering with drunken bees.
It blooms every year this time
like the clockwork of
the hardest kind
of hope.)

Abandoned Car

He hurled his watch into the one bit of water he'd seen,
single glop shaking the pollen-filmed surface for only
a stark few Swiss-steel-Self-winding-Jewel-pivot seconds
before stillness settled onto the edges like silence.

Later, wrist-rubbing, he caught himself wondering the time,
the sun pinned bold to the blue like a hole on a silkscreen,
crackling the mud into angled plates, concave curls of clay
crumbling so brittle beneath the easing weight of his socks.

Double-breasted jacket javelined away, he has towelled
his dress shirt over his scalp to block the slow sizzle out,
breathing in vivid colours and air as sharp as needles,
he greets a lizard by name as it scuttles for cover.

Stopping on the crest of a dune to scout, hand on his brow,
a sweep of the gasoline-vapour skyline, squint-frown,
a sigh, smack on the roof of his mouth with a tongue gone dry,
he measures in flights of a crow, still nudging him: go, man, go.

Abandoned Resort

As the tourist trickle dries
proprietors' dusty sighs soon
orphan their streets to twiddle
the breezy thumbs of plastic bags

With doors bolted and left for dead
storms test the shutters and whisper
cold insults through their weaknesses
Winter sun blinding the paint of signs

Spiders revel in the dark of white spaces
weaving shrines to the god of porcelain precision
Weeds spill over the brims of window planters
flaunting the heights with a view to die for

Earwigs circle as if in disbelief
the bottom rim of a marmalade jar
its motherlode seepage of nectar, while
moths swim unbound through cotton oceans

What was once a vacation haven – solitude
of short-lived sagas and containered delight –
is now a microcosm of similar thrills
The kind you take when you can get

Abandoned Toys

they were the most valuable things we had
so, on parting that summer, it made sense
to bury them
as conquistadors might their bullion
before crossing an ocean
in doubtful times

it was in the tinkling shade of a birch
in a cleft at the trunk
plastic soldiers placed methodically
into a hand-dug foxhole
on their backs and lined up
like a platoon ready for inspection

with ceremony we spread the first layer
of soil, letting it sift through our fingers
then the clay, packing it down tight
with our palms

i'm sure they're still there
in their moulded fatigues
postures hunched, barrels raised
threateningly, while rhizomes and
root hair thread between their legs
gently finger their helmeted heads

but like most things buried too long
i've forgotten how to reach them
which, if i'm not mistaken
is what makes a treasure

Abandoned Grave

A country walk in southern England
everything smudged in green with a
friend whose eyes (like everyone in
his village) are the same bruised colour
of the sea murmuring a few miles off

We ate tidily sliced sandwiches
of white bread and sat on a stone bench
smudged in green (like every bench
in the area) chatting about
the cemetery that sloped away

We would eventually walk through
its rows and find a headstone tilting
to the side (like every tomb on
the hill) whose engravings had been
sanded away by the sea-winds and rain

And we made irreverent comments
and hard-luck stories to chuckle out
our sombreness (like every English-
man does) and walked away from the
unmarkings of this listing tombstone

which seemed to be slowly sinking
into the ground of smudging green as
if it were a bruised sea (like every
sea is) thinking to myself that what does
remain of this grave is the colour of its eyes

Carpenter Ant

Something had to be wrong with it
Middle of the day, winter, and here it was
walking the length of the apartment's
impossible prairie of hardwood
Wasn't moving like an ant should either
no pauses to smell or taste or
whatever they do, it was simply
plodding along, straight ahead, blind
to the three cats, one dog, and human
it was passing between, all of us
following it gradually across the floor

Living in a house of wood
I should've killed it, and was half-
waiting for one of the animals to
every one of which I'd seen pounce
their lion's share of insects

None of us budged
which made me think of
Alzheimer's patients wandering out
into the streets of a snowy night
or returning soldiers gone mad
or even friends in their mid-life crises
Something surrendering itself wholly
recklessly, out to a universe that
the rest of us understood
just as little about

The male cat, intrepid hunter
of the lot, watched the ant until
it was lost in the wooden distance
let out a sigh, and turned his head

Discovering Smallness

for Jeff Doherty

I could barely vote, and you could not
when we set out into the wilderness
bringing only
too much of what we didn't need

Heads bent into the rain
we were invincible, spry, wise
sensing the edges of the wild
shrinking back as we passed

Weeks whittled themselves away
before we came across the perfect trail
not yet even drawn on our maps
moving deep into the nature
of our aspirations

Poetry in mind we took it
heads bent into the rain
and three days later had walked off the map
the path petering out, and were without
enough food to go back the way we came

We lit a small, sober fire
The night towered over the trees
coveting its uncharted valleys
all the forsaken corners
of its reign

Years would pass
we'd lose touch, both of us
falling down on our separate ways
Both getting to our feet again

Yet I often think of that meagre pile of sticks
to that feeling of inextinguishable warmth
slipping between our fingers there
the unknowable dark unravelling
beyond the tiny light of our fireside
and about the part of us, in that place,
that never left

Camino de Santiago

I have walked over a thousand kilometres
to reach this shore, following a path over
a thousand years old

And it's the same as it's always been
It is the miles we amble
not running from anything
not searching for anything
that we find

The Shades of Your Black

haunt me
gruff voices that sift
through windows and doors
conjuring shapes
of a twisted cawing in winter trees
blotches like spilt ink
on a blurry screen of branches

Only when the quiet unfurls
do I know you've dropped into the air
and are sweeping out
over power lines and rooftops
leaving a trail of straggling bleats and cackles
that swirl around heating ducts
the scratch of your wings
raking through the mist
and sending cats scuttling for cover
Until, circling the outskirts like a funnel cloud
you land on the ragged remains
of crucified strawmen
while they shrug dejectedly
at their own ineptitude

Haunted
because all I want
is what you have
freedom so pure it's invisible
To dare, flee, wander, find,
evoke such stirring in this world
just by passing through it
blind

Fireside Conversation

We happened upon them
by accident of perfect timing,
seven days into the endless boreal
wetlands of northern Ontario.
Thank god someone knew how
rare they were, dragonfly chrysalides
emerging from their last skin, neon
nakedness shimmering against dull
stone. She explained, leaning out
over the bow of her canoe, the various
stages of their life cycle, how in every
phase they were voracious, formidable
predators, as they would be again in only
a few minutes, once their wings, wet from
their latest birth, were crisp enough to fly.
Until then they were wholly susceptible.
We fell into silence, staring, transfixed, into
their glassy-blue fire, waiting for them to dry.

Then tonight that rough man who did the
rototilling dropped by for his money
and I reluctantly offered him some wine
that he accepted and sat stiffly by the hearth
to drink, saying little until he started in on his
wife, gone this time last year. And when
his voice broke I glanced up astounded
to see how glassy blue his eyes were
and then stared quickly back into the fire
waiting for them to dry.

A Crab on Vargas Island

Sitting around the fire you asked me
    what I was thinking   I said nothing
        which wasn't true
    On my walk before dark I noticed something
wriggling between two corrugations in the strand
    an orphan on the tarmac of wave-shattered shells
        It was lying on its back, legs kicking in a slowing
        battle to right its white belly
        globule eyes staring up into the sand
            Pinching one of its legs I hurled it
out at the surf where it thumped onto the receding
    waterline   upside-down again   and left it there, tiny
        treadmilling the air in the dull sheet-metal light
    another waylaid error for the tide to make right
sweep its sable-slate clean
            Yet it was just big enough
    to be something else
I wouldn't mention

Ninth Street North

Lane of my upbringing, pickup-truck lined, their hollow backs
　　polished to a gleam or rusting slow, exposed tire-rims pinned
　　onto wooden blocks, a limping-crutch advance through the wind
to as right a season can be on the wrong side of tracks.

Sun dangling bald from an unseen wire, gestapo-bulb sway
　　staring everything down with a kitchen-window glare,
　　crosshatching shade, casting etches in grass-knotted care
as if memorizing the forms of things for a rainy day.

There's the alley where, distracted, I meandered to school
　　hurried along by the bell's shaky electronic bleat,
　　the stunted dark of my shadow chasing wild at my feet,
only to wait for me there at the door, obedient fool.

Here's the lawn where I knelt plucking geodesic domes
　　of dandelion heads from lactating stalks, wispy down
　　umbrellas spinning away, hurricane-pucker blown
to land on the neighbour's, who'd shoo me off to other homes.

Duplex of boyhood friends, quiet mailboxes, rusty hinges,
　　the still fog of curtains inhaling the secrets of rooms
　　like children holding their breath before crawling through
the suspension of aqua-tiled chlorine, blurring the fringes.

A sidewalk that gleams more exotic each time I'm back,
　　and notice the obtuse shadow stomping with my gait,
　　its feet pressing up on my gum-smeared soles with a weight
equal to mine, as if holding me up, as if keeping track.

Nonna

Sometimes you talk to the dead
who understand how things
are capable of vanishing
from places you would swear –
and on the Virgin Mary –
you put them. Words on the edge
of your tongue so   close.

The more your world faded
the more I unfairly asked you
to recall its details, waiting while you
squinted into the receding dark
where the dead gazed back,
endlessly searching for signs
of love they left behind
and at times reaching forward
to steal mementos from it.

Before they were lost, I had you cook
my favourite recipes, manically noting quantities
(lavish generously with olive oil; fist of salt)
watching your beautiful weathered hands.

One day in your garden, you told me of
your grandmother, back in your tiny village
in Italy, who always kept a particular
kind of flower growing, a yellow one
in memory of her own Nonna.
I asked what kind it was exactly
and watched your eyes floating
through salt water
back to Calabria.

But the name wasn't growing
where it used to (the dead
shuffled their feet) and could
only be remembered halfway.

So I poke seeds into clay pots
trying to remember for you
the half that is missing.
But, like your recipes, never quite
seem to get it exactly right,
though sense, at times,
that I am so
close.

Unearthing Another Temple

This is long, long after you,
though once it was your kitchen.
Some of your cutlery is still in
the drawers, artifacts that will help us
learn how you lived, elucidate
your day-to-day routines.

Small animals skitter along
the warpings of your floorboards,
beneath the counter with its matted heap
of leaf litter; tendrils of green sprouts
spiking through the detritus, the tiny
lobes of their heads bowing.

Your cupboard doors lie open
or unhinged, spilling soil, strung with
the kinking yarn of vines and stratified foliage.
The windows are gone and sighing
with open air, though a half-buried
coffee cup – your favourite – rises

from the dirt on a collapsing sill,
tilting out to the forest canopy,
mouthing an expressive O. The corner
of the room has been pried open
by the rippling muscle of a tree root,
having wormed its way in from the ceiling,

where there is now a hole, allowing the sun
(which in your time could only shaft inside
on select mornings over the winter) to freely
explore the uneven ground, a slow sweep
of warmth that fingers whatever it chooses,
peeking in from its belly on the roof
like a god.

How to Make a Cake from Scratch

First you will need to take out your recipe,
as well as every recipe you've ever been given
and burn them. It is critical you disregard
anything anyone has ever told you about making
cake. A jerry can of gasoline and match facilitate.

The ingredients are complex. They will change
when you wish they would not. Avoid gathering
all your favourite tastes and textures. If you do so
the overall flavour will be bland and lack colour.
A zest of lemon in some form or another is best.

Your oven will need stoking, so you must leave
the comfort of your home, and go to the place that you
have been advised never to go. It is a place where the wood
is hard, the soil precarious, the air volatile. Go there.
Stand thin at its centre. Now close your eyes. And begin.

I Used to Believe

That there was a portal in my closet
to another world,
and that my mother's washing machine
was haunted.

That we were all assigned
guardian angels
who balanced
precariously
on treetops
watching over us
at every hour. And
when you heard your name in a crowd
and spun around to find
no one,
it was, in fact, one of them,
speaking – by accident –
out loud.

And that taxidermied heads blinked in the
floating dust of attics and basements.
That autumn trees turned colour because,
like everything,
there was something inside them
that was on fire,
and that their blushing with it
somehow smouldered
into ignition.

Once upon a time
I believed in science too.
That questions were posed
to be answered. That
conviction
was a strength.

And also in grace, in balance, in order.

That journeys were always long,
and that struggle
was something
that drained you.

I used to believe
that beliefs
would never fold in on themselves,
that once the fire was gone
from the theory,
it could never find its way
back
into the leaves.

It's true. There really was a time
when I believed that the last
word of a poem
was where it
ended.

About the Author

The multi-talented Mark Lavorato was raised on the Canadian Prairies, but has spent most of his adult life living, working, and writing on his travels throughout Central and North America, the Caribbean, and Europe. He was inspired to write while living in the Austrian Alps, reflecting on unsettling true stories he'd heard in the jungles of Guatemala. Aside from his writing, Mark is also a photographer and composer. (http://www.marklavorato.com)

A Note on the Type

This book is typeset in Junius. The typeface is named for Franciscus Junius, a pioneer of Germanic philology who was born at Heidelberg in 1591.

The typeface was digitized in the early 1990s from the Pica Saxon used to print Georges Hickes' *Thesaurus* (Oxford: Sheldonian Theatre, 1703–05). Junius is primarily designed for use by medievalists, and is readily available for download from the English Department at the University of Virginia.